Rabbits' Habits

A book about good habits

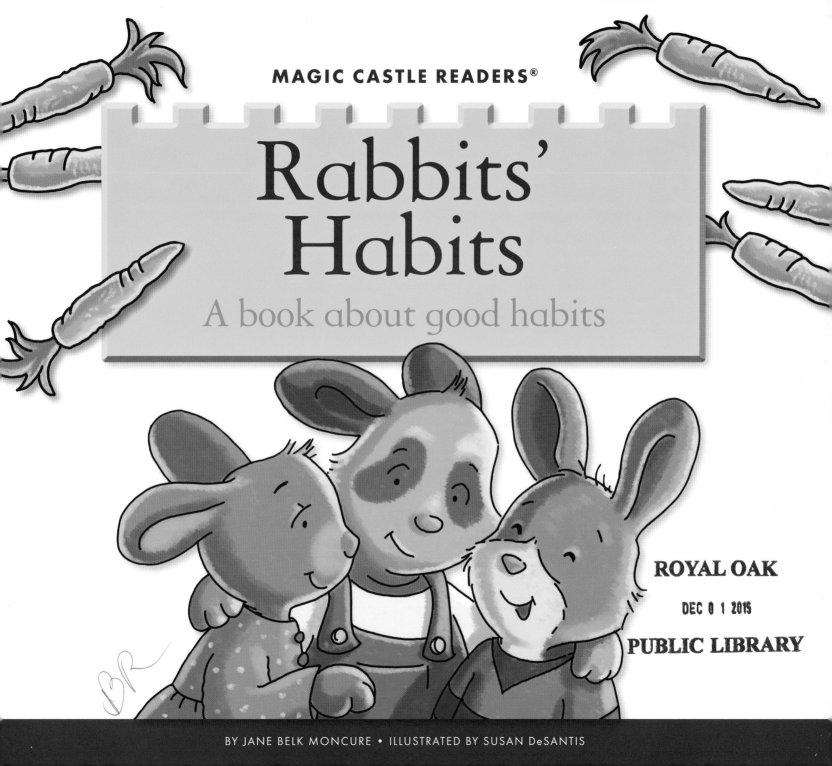

BY JANE BELK MONCURE • ILLUSTRATED BY SUSAN DeSANTIS

The Child's World

Published by The Child's World®
1980 Lookout Drive • Mankato, MN 56003-1705
800-599-READ • www.childsworld.com

Acknowledgments
The Child's World®: Mary Berendes, Publishing Director
The Design Lab: Design
Jody Jensen Shaffer: Editing
Derrick Chow: Color

ISBN 9781623235697
LCCN 2013931365

Printed in the United States of America
Mankato, MN
July 2013
PA02177

Did you know...

A library is a magic castle with many Word Windows in it?

What is a Word Window?

If you said, "A book," you're right!

A book is a Word Window because the words and pictures let you look and see many things. Books are your windows to the wide, wide world around you.

The Library
Is a Magic Castle

Come to the Magic Castle
When you are growing tall.
Rows and rows of Word Windows
Line every single wall.
They reach up high,
As high as the sky,
And you'll want to open them all.
For every time you open one,
A new adventure has begun.

3

Sara opened a Word Window.
Here is what she read:

Once there were three little rabbits.

The first little rabbit had a habit
of dropping his things here and there.

The second rabbit had a habit
of leaving her things everywhere.

The third rabbit had a habit
of putting his things where they belonged.

Which rabbit had a good habit?

One day, the three little rabbits hopped to the park to play.

One rabbit had a habit of pushing and punching
to get her way.

One rabbit had a habit of pulling and pinching
so he could be first in line.

But one rabbit had a habit of waiting his turn.

Which little rabbit had a good habit?

One day, Papa Rabbit said,
"Let's plant a garden."
He gave each little rabbit some garden tools.

The first rabbit stayed in the wheelbarrow.
"I will not," he said. He had a habit of
saying this.

The second rabbit started to dig.
"I cannot," she said. She had a habit of
saying this.

The third rabbit said, "Come on. Let's go!"
He went right to work and finished the job.

Which little rabbit had a good habit?

When Monday came, it was time to get up and go to school.

One rabbit had a habit of going to bed on time.
She woke up on time. She was ready when the
school bus came.

One rabbit had a habit of staying up late.
He was too tired in the morning.
He missed the school bus.

One rabbit had a habit of playing instead of
getting ready. He missed the school bus, too.

Which little rabbit had a good habit?

At school, the little rabbits had a race.
One rabbit cried because he did not win.
He had a habit of crying.

One rabbit frowned because she did not win.
She had a habit of frowning.

One rabbit did not win, but he still smiled.
"I will try again," he said. "Maybe I will win
next time."

Which little rabbit had a good habit?

The three little rabbits hopped to the school picnic.
Do you know why they were all smiling?

All three rabbits had the same habit.
Can you guess what it was?

The rabbits ate good food. They ate fruits and vegetables. What a nice rabbit habit!

Questions and Activities

(Write your answers on a sheet of paper.)

1. Name two good habits you learned about in this story.
    What other good habits would you like to know about?

2. Did this story have any words you don't know?
    How can you find out what they mean?

3. Look at the picture on page 13.
    What does it show about having good habits?

4. Why did the third rabbit miss the school bus?
    Why was he not ready when the school bus came?

5. Tell this story to a friend. Take only two minutes.
    Which parts did you share?